The Arbitration Game

Louis V. Imundo

Arbitrator

ISBN: 0-538-07690-9

LIBRARY OF CONGRESS CATALOG
CARD NUMBER: 80-54765

Printed in the United States of America

1 2 3 4 5 6 7 K 7 6 5 4 3 2 1

Published by

G69 SOUTH-WESTERN PUBLISHING CO.

CINCINNATI   WEST CHICAGO, ILL.   DALLAS   PELHAM MANOR, N.Y.   PALO ALTO, CALIF.

The Players

TEAM PLAYERS FOR MANAGEMENT

Frank J. Edwards, Vice President, Human Resources
Robert Clark, Manager, Machine Department
Terry Schrickel, Assistant to Frank Edwards
Dennis Cushing, Supervisor, Machine Department
Sarah Engels, Supervisor, Machine Department
Jim Phillips, Ex-Employee

TEAM PLAYERS FOR THE UNION

Charles Constable, International Representative, UBAW
Evelyn Stout, Chief Steward, Local 209, UBAW
Sam Nielson, Steward
Lillian Rattison, Steward
Mark Osborne, Employee and Character Witness for Grievant
Raymond Butler, Employee and Character Witness for Grievant
Robert M. Jones, Grievant

PANEL OF ARBITRATORS

Dr. Michael Rothstein, Arbitrator Picked by the Company
Dr. Katherine Gibson, Arbitrator Picked by the Union
Dr. Curtis Redstone, Arbitrator Jointly Agreed upon by the Parties

The Arbitration Game

The Arbitration Game you are about to participate in was developed to help students of labor-management relations and practitioners who represent either labor or management increase their effectiveness in preparing and presenting cases before arbitrators. The game centers around a long-term employee who was discharged by management for chronic misbehavior and an inability to respond in a positive manner to previous corrective disciplinary efforts. Discharge cases represent the type of case most frequently heard by arbitrators. Arbitrators derive their authority to decide cases of conflict between employees and their employers from arbitration clauses in negotiated labor-management agreements. In most labor-management agreements, the authority of the arbitrator is final and binding on the parties to the agreement, or what is commonly referred to as the contract.

Until recently, appeals from arbitrators' decisions were extremely rare. However, with the passage of civil rights legislation, and, in general, the increasing propensity of people to sue one another, appeals of arbitrators' decisions have become more frequent. Employees, in increasing numbers, are exercising their rights to sue both employers and unions. The increased risk of further litigation, perhaps more than anything else, has served to motivate representatives of both labor and management to prepare more thoroughly for arbitration, and for that matter any other type of legal or quasi-legal proceeding.

Assuming that a case to be arbitrated has merit in the eyes of labor and management, the outcome of an arbitration proceeding can be significantly influenced by the quality of the parties' preparation and presentation of their respective cases. Considerable skill is required in properly preparing and presenting a case. In general, the side that best prepares its case or game plan and most effectively executes it is the side that is most likely to get the decision it sought.

As a participant in the game representing either *labor* or *management*, you have been given information to assist you and your fellow team members in developing and presenting your case. Your team must carefully review the available information, and based upon that information, prepare and present a case. A panel of three arbitrators has been selected to hear the case, and information is given about the training and experience of each. Knowledge of arbitrators' backgrounds and experiences can be important in formulating strategy and tactics for presenting a case.

The arbitrators have been charged with the responsibility of guiding the conduct of the proceeding. After both parties have concluded their presentations, the arbitrators will review the testimony of the parties and render a binding decision.

The group will have an opportunity to critique the entire game and the behavior of participants after the arbitrators' decision has been made known.

Selecting Arbitrators and Assessing Their Competency or Impartiality

Most large unions have a department in their national headquarters whose responsibility it is to secure and evaluate feedback from field office personnel who participate in arbitration proceedings. Compared to management, union representatives tend to be better informed about the credentials, experience, and quality of judgment of arbitrators. Unions carefully review arbitrators' published decisions to develop an understanding about how a particular arbitrator judges a case and arrives at a decision. Based upon their evaluations, they recommend which arbitrators should be selected for specific types of cases.

Most managers do not have the inclination nor the time to read and comprehensively analyze arbitrators' published decisions. Some managers, either through industry associations or personal contacts, are able to learn about the perceived competency or impartiality of arbitrators. Most, however, use the services of attorneys, consultants, or organizations who specialize in reviewing arbitrators' decisions. These people or groups either review and analyze published decisions or rely upon the feedback of others who participate in arbitration proceedings.

Approximately 10 to 15 percent of the rendered arbitration decisions are printed in their complete texts. Some sources of published decisions are the Bureau of National Affairs Labor Relations Reports, Commerce Clearing House's American Labor Arbitration Awards, Prentice-Hall Reports, and the Labor Relations Press Reports.

The following general guidelines are used in evaluating arbitrators:

- How soon after the close of the arbitration hearing was the decision awarded? Was it within the preferred 30 days? If not, was there a justifiable reason for its taking longer?

- How was the issue decided?

- Did the arbitrator consider only relevant contractual provisions or was weight given to other matters, such as the practices and customs of the parties, history of practices under the agreement, etc.?

- Did the arbitrator follow the concept that management rights are residual; that is, all rights and privileges of managing the business continue to reside with the employer except to the extent they have been abridged, modified, or compromised by provisions or interpretations of the agreement?

- Was the hearing conducted in a formal or informal manner?

- Did the arbitrator prefer a transcript of the hearing and use of a stenographer or simply take notes?

- Did the arbitrator rule on objections, or accept all evidence and testimony proffered by the parties?

- Did the arbitrator ask many questions to gain a clear understanding of testimony, or did the testimony given suffice?

- In the opinion portion of the award, were the arbitrator's remarks pertinent and to the point or were they vague? Did the arbitrator delve into extraneous and foreign matters that were submitted or tendered?

- Was the written opinion and award clear and understandable?

- Were the arbitrator's fees reasonable?

The Company

The ABC Company is a large producer of machined steel products. Its primary operations are carried on at a single location in Michigan. The company was founded in the late 1800s and has grown to an annual dollar volume of 350 million per year. It employs over 1600 people in its various operating departments. One of the largest departments is the Machine Department, where forgings, castings, stampings, and the like are machined to either rough or finished dimensions.

The people who work in the Machine Department are semiskilled to highly skilled machinists. The highest job classification is the Set-Up Machinist. The Set-Up Machinist is responsible for insuring that work to be machined is properly set up on a lathe before any operations are performed, and in addition oversees the machining of difficult work in process. It takes many years and considerable skill to become a Set-Up Machinist.

Employees in the Machine Department work various shifts on a rotating basis, their hours being based on manufacturing schedules.

The Union

Local 209 of the United Brotherhood of American Workers represents all of the hourly paid employees at the primary operations center of The ABC Company. The union organized the company in 1959. Labor-management relations between the company and the union can be described as harmonious. The union has struck the company once since it was organized.

While grievances are frequently filed by employees, the majority are settled without having to resort to arbitration. On the average, only one or two cases are arbitrated each year. The union has won about half of the cases.

The union's negotiating committee is comprised of three very aggressive and capable employees. The union's international representative is an experienced labor-management relations expert. Relations between the international's regional office and the local are good.

The current labor-management agreement is a three-year agreement due to expire in fourteen months. The agreement contains a union shop clause applicable to all members of the bargaining unit.

Biographical Profiles

Frank J. Edwards, Vice President, Human Resources

Edwards is in his early forties and has been with the company since 1967. He holds an advanced degree in personnel management and has a reputation for being capable, fair, and honest. He feels that the company has gone the distance in trying to rehabilitate Jones. In addition, he feels that Jones is a troublemaker and winning this arbitration would go a long way toward reducing some of the problems in the Machine Department.

Robert Clark, Manager, Machine Department

Clark is in his early fifties and has been with the company since 1970. He is a capable manager and has a reputation for getting things accomplished. He respects the union, although he wishes that it were not present at all. When he took over the Department, Jones was one of his first problems. He feels that Jones is a troublemaker and has wanted to get rid of him for some time. He feels that the company, and Edwards in particular, has been soft on discipline.

Terry Schrickel, Assistant to Frank Edwards

Schrickel is a recent college graduate who joined the company three years ago. He rapidly became Edwards' right arm. He is enrolled in an evening law school program and has taken a number of courses in labor law and labor-management relations.

Dennis Cushing and Sarah Engels, Supervisors, Machine Department

Cushing and Engels are department supervisors. Both are in their late forties and have been employed at the company since 1965. Both came up from the ranks and have completed high school. Both have supervised the grievant over the years. They regard him as a highly skilled machinist but feel that he is a troublemaker. They are afraid of him because of his reputation and try to avoid interacting with him. They are a little concerned about possibly having to testify about Jones before the arbitrators.

Charles Constable, International Representative, UBAW

Constable is a seasoned labor-management relations veteran. He has a reputation for winning arbitrations. His personal relationship with Local 209 has not been the best, and he would like to win this case because that would increase his influence and prestige with the local union's negotiating committee.

Evelyn Stout, Chief Steward, Local 209, UBAW

Stout has been the chief steward for the past three years. She is up for re-election in three months and is being challenged by a number of the union's members. Jones can influence a lot of votes, and winning this case for Jones would insure her reelection. A defeat would virtually guarantee the loss of her bid for reelection.

Sam Nielson and Lillian Rattison, Stewards

Nielson and Rattison have been stewards for a number of years. They are sympathetic to Jones because of his age and seniority with the company. They also fear that if his discharge is upheld by the arbitrators, Jones will file misrepresentation charges against the union. They also fear that Jones' friends will seek revenge against the negotiating committee for a loss.

Mark Osborne and Raymond Butler, Employees

Both Osborne and Butler are old friends of the grievant. They have been employed by the company for sixteen and eighteen years respectively. They feel that the company is in part responsible for Jones' problems because for years they overworked him. They are not above lying to help Jones save his job. Osborne and Butler have good work records, although they are suspected by management of being the leaders of a theft ring that has plagued the company for some time.

Jim Phillips, Ex-Employee

Jim Phillips is the company's principal witness in this arbitration hearing. He quit the company in October 1980. He is presently working for another firm and is voluntarily testifying against the grievant. His reason for quitting was that he was "being pressured by other employees," namely, the grievant and his friends.

Phillips was employed by the company for two years. At best, he was an average employee. His attendance barely met the minimum requirements and he rarely exerted himself to produce beyond the minimum expected of him. The only disciplinary actions taken against him were a couple of warnings for bad attendance.

Robert M. Jones, Grievant

Age: 56

Marital Status: Married with children (grown and not living at home)

Employment Date: January 1952

Health: Fair to good. However, he admits that he is an alcoholic.

Education: Eighth grade. Has completed numerous machinist training courses over the years.

Robert M. Jones, the grievant, holds the highest job classification in the Machine Department of The ABC Company and is one of the most highly skilled employees. Although he has a limited formal education, he knows his work backwards and forwards. In addition, he is street smart.

Until about 1972 Jones had an excellent record as an employee. In fact, he had been offered a supervisory position on a number of occasions. Each time he refused the promotion. Sometime in 1971 it became evident that Jones had a drinking problem. Over the years since then, Jones' behavior has progressively deteriorated.

Jones is a rough sort of man and had a reputation as a fighter during his youth. It is known, although it cannot be proven, that Jones has beaten or threatened a number of employees. Jones' present friends in the employ of the company can be best described as troublesome. Jones is not above lying to avoid getting into or out of trouble.

Blackburn, Smith & Kagel

Attorneys at Law
1525 Crestview Square
Detroit, MI 48236

December 1, 1980

Mr. Frank J. Edwards
Vice President, Human Resources
The ABC Company
Evans, MI 48616

Dear Mr. Edwards:

We have completed our review of the panel of arbitrators submitted to you by the American Arbitration Association from which arbitrators are to be selected to hear the Robert M. Jones discharge case. Considering the importance of this case to the company, we recommend you select Dr. Michael Rothstein as the "company selected arbitrator." Dr. Rothstein is one of the most experienced and capable arbitrators in this region. He tends to be a strict disciplinarian and is more inclined to support management on discharge cases. During the past year he rendered 63 decisions. Thirty-nine were in management's favor.

One point to remember: he thinks in a highly legalistic and organized manner. If evidence or testimony is not properly introduced, he will either reject it outright or fail to give it any weight when making a decision.

In our opinion, the union will select Dr. Katherine Gibson as the "union selected arbitrator." Dr. Gibson, although not as experienced as others on the list, is very capable. She rendered 14 decisions this past year. Ten were in favor of the grievant(s). She is somewhat egalitarian in her views and believes unions are necessary in order to keep management from mistreating employees. Her judgment is excellent and she writes an excellent decision.

In all likelihood the "neutral" panel member will be Dr. Curtis Redstone. He is experienced and competent. The union, for a variety of reasons, will reject the others listed on the panel. We recommend that you do the same pursuant to the alternate striking procedure outlined in your labor-management agreement.

Sincerely,

Mark A. Blackburn
Attorney

MAB/se

Arbitrators' Biographical Profiles

Dr. Michael Rothstein

Dr. Rothstein was selected by the Company.

Occupation:	Attorney, Arbitrator, Professor of Law
Business Address:	640 Century Building Suite 3706 Detroit, MI 48126
Professional Affiliations:	National Academy of Arbitration American Arbitration Association Federal Mediation & Conciliation Service American Bar Association American Trial Lawyers Association
Experience:	Arbitrator, Professor of Labor Law, Attorney in private practice

Issue. New or reopened contract terms, contract interpretation, discharge and disciplinary action, incentive rates or standards, job evaluation, promotion and upgrading, layoff, bumping and recall, transfer, seniority, overtime pay, overtime distribution, compulsory overtime, union officers, union business, strike or lockout, vacations, vacation pay, holidays, holiday pay, work scheduling, reporting, callin-callback pay, health and welfare, pensions, other fringe benefits, subcontracting, jurisdictional disputes, agreement scope: supervision, etc., mergers, consolidations, severance pay.

Industry. Agriculture, aluminum, automotive, aerospace, bakery, beverage, brass and copper, brewery, broadcasting, canning, retail and chain stores, chemicals, clothing, coal, communications, constructions, dairy products, distillery, electrical equipment, electrical appliances, feed and fertilizer, foundry, gas and electric power, glass, grain mill, heating and ventilation, scientific instrument, insurance, lumber, machinery, nonelectrical, manufacturing, maritime, meat packing, metal fabrications, nonferrous metals, paint and varnish, pharmaceutical, petroleum, plastics, plumbing fixtures, printing and publishing, rubber, steel, food.

Education:	B.S., Economics, Notre Dame, 1946 LLB, Law, Fordan Law School, 1950 LLM, Law, Michigan Law School, 1956 JSD, Law, Michigan Law School, 1968
Certification:	Attorney, New York, 1950 Attorney, Michigan, 1955
Per Diem Fee:	$400
Year of Birth:	1925

Dr. Katherine Gibson

Dr. Gibson was selected by the Union.

Occupation:	Professor, Arbitrator
Business Address:	12 Brunswick Hall
	Barons College
	Casper, MI 49913
Professional Affiliations:	American Arbitration Association
	Federal Mediation & Conciliation Service
Experience:	Office Manager — Derek Corporation
	Training Coordinator — Sears, Roebuck & Co.
	Professor — Cleveland State University

Issue. Contract interpretation, discharge and disciplinary action, incentive rates or standards, job evaluation, layoff, bumping and recall, seniority, overtime pay, overtime distribution, union officers, union business, strike or lockout, vacations, vacation pay, holidays, holiday pay, jurisdictional disputes, job classification, discrimination, job posting and bidding, assignment of work.

Industry. Aluminum, retail and chain stores, chemical, communications, distillery, electrical appliances, foundry, furniture, gas and electric power, manufacturing, metal fabrications, paint and varnish, plastics, printing and publishing, pulp and paper products, shoe, steel, textile, transportation.

Education:	B.A., Philosophy, University of Kentucky, 1962
	M.A., Sociology, University of Dayton, 1966
	Ph.D., Political Science, Michigan State University, 1973
Certification:	None
Per Diem Fee:	$350
Year of Birth:	1940

Dr. Curtis Redstone

Dr. Redstone was selected by both parties.

Occupation:	Professor, Consultant, Arbitrator
Business Address:	264 Randell Hall
	Grinch State University
	Mayville, MI 48744
Professional Affiliations:	National Academy of Arbitration
	American Arbitration Association
	Federal Mediation & Conciliation Service
Experience:	Industrial Engineer — Grumman Corp.
	Manager, Industrial Engineering — Boeing Corp.
	Arbitrator, State of Michigan

Issue. Contract interpretation, discharge and disciplinary action, incentive rates or standards, job evaluation, overtime pay, overtime distribution, compulsory overtime, strike or lockout, vacations, vacation pay, holidays, holiday pay, work scheduling, reporting, callin-callback pay, health and welfare, pensions, other fringe benefits, subcontracting.

Industry. Electrical equipment, electrical appliances, foundry, furniture, gas, and electric power, glass, lumber, machinery, nonelectrical, manufacturing, metal fabrications, nonferrous metals, plastics, plumbing fixtures, printing and publishing, pulp and paper products, rubber, steel, stone, quarry, textile, transportation, trucking and storage, other.

Education:	B.S., Industrial Engineering, New York University, 1942
	M.B.A., Business Administration, Wayne State University, 1953
	Ph.D., Economics, Labor, Management, University of Pennsylvania, 1962
Certification:	Professional Engineer, 1950
Per Diem Fee:	$400
Year of Birth:	1920

The ABC Company
Company Rules

The rules and regulations listed herein shall govern the conduct and safety of all plant employees of the company. Wherever a large number of persons work together, rules are needed to insure proper teamwork. These rules shall remain in full force and effect until canceled, supplemented, or amended by the company.

A baseball or a football player who violates a rule of the game draws a penalty in keeping with the seriousness of the offense. Those who fail to observe our rules are subject to disciplinary action, too. Penalties, likewise, depend upon the seriousness of the violation. The company has not in the past, and will not in the future, deal out penalties without looking into the matter impartially. A written warning will not be charged against an employee for over two (2) years from the date of such written warning.

Committing any of the following violations will be sufficient grounds for disciplinary action ranging from written reprimand to immediate suspension with intent to discharge, depending upon the seriousness of the offense in the judgment of the company. The anticipated disciplinary action for the first offense of the company rules is as follows:

A. Written Reprimand

1. Absence without reasonable or justifiable cause.

2. Reporting late for work.

Employees reporting for work late will be offered their regular job if it is operating, or any available work if that job is not operating, providing at least one half of the scheduled shift is worked, not counting lunch.

Employees who report for work 4 or more minutes late at the start of the shift or who work 4 or more minutes less than a full quarter hour at quitting time will be docked ¼ of an hour's pay.

3. If an employee is absent, the reason for the absence and the expected time of return to work must be reported to the supervisor no later than the end of the first shift that has not been worked, or the employee must be able to fully justify the reason for any failure to report.

4. On overtime or premium days, such report of absence and the expected time of return to work must be given to the supervisor no later than one hour before the start of the overtime shift in order that a replacement may be scheduled, or the employee must be able to fully justify the reason for any failure to report.

5. Leaving the plant for claimed medical reasons after work has been assigned to an employee and the shift has begun, must be supported either by furnishing proof, or by obvious necessity, or the employee's absence will be considered unjustified.

6. Creating or contributing to unsanitary conditions.

7. Making scrap unnecessarily, or careless workmanship.

8. Wasting time or loitering during working hours. (Employees outside their own working hours are considered visitors.)

9. Smoking in restricted areas.

10. Unauthorized soliciting or collecting contributions for any purpose whatsoever during working hours.

11. Unauthorized distribution of literature, written or printed matter of any description, in work areas or on company premises during working hours.

12. Posting or removal of notices, signs, or writing in any form on bulletin boards or on company property at anytime.

13. Gambling, lottery, or any other game of chance on company premises at anytime.

14. Failure to maintain acceptable standards of production and/or quality.

15. Assignment of wages or frequent garnishments.

B. Written Reprimand to Three (3) Days Disciplinary Layoff

1. Leaving the plant during working hours without permission.

2. Distracting the attention of others, or causing confusion by unnecessary shouting, catcalls, or demonstration in the plant.

3. Unauthorized operation of machines, tools, or equipment.

4. Horseplay, scuffling, running, or throwing things.

C. Written Reprimand to One (1) Week Disciplinary Layoff

1. Abusive language to any employee or supervisor.

2. Possession of, or being under the influence of, intoxicants or drugs on company property to the extent that the employee cannot function safely or efficiently.

3. Disregard for, or violation of, safety rules or common safety practices.

D. Written Reprimand to Discharge

1. Falsification of personnel or other records.

2. Ringing the clock card of another employee or falsely reporting own time.

3. Possession of weapons on company premises at anytime without permission.

4. Refusal to obey instructions or orders of supervisors, or refusal to do a job assignment. (Do the work assigned to you and follow instructions. Any complaint may be taken up later through the regular channels.)

5. Threatening, intimidating, coercing, or interfering with employees or supervisors at anytime.

6. Abuse, misuse, deliberate destruction, theft, or misappropriation of company property, tools, equipment, or the property of employees or customers, in any manner.

7. Fighting on the premises at anytime.

8. Immoral conduct or indecency.

Repeated violations of these rules will subject an employee to increased penalty, depending upon the nature, severity, and timeliness of the offense. Also, multiple violation of the above rule categories may result in disciplinary action up to and including suspension for cumulative misconduct. Should an employee be suspended, the result may be either discharge or return to the employee's original job, depending upon the decision of the company pursuant to Article 14 of the contract.

The ABC Company
Safety Rules

Your safety and welfare is of the greatest concern, but no matter what or how much the company may provide in the way of safety devices, such efforts will not be truly effective unless you consider the safety program as part of your individual responsibility. Here are some of the rules which must be observed:

1. Always remember that safety is insured by vigilance, watchfulness, and common sense. Never assume that caution will be exercised by others when your own safety is involved; and when in doubt, ask questions.

2. Employees must wear steel-toed safety shoes, safety glasses, and a safety hat while on the job.

3. Never set any machinery in motion without first making sure that no one is in a position to be injured. If safety guards are provided, do not operate the machine unless the guards are in place.

4. Place stock or material in the proper places. Before you leave, be sure the material is piled or blocked up safely. Keep aisles and exits open at all times.

5. Do not try to lift, pull, or push loads in an improper fashion or that are too heavy for you. When you do lift, bend your knees and keep your back as straight as possible; then push up with your legs.

6. Most accidents can be prevented by just ordinary good common sense and good housekeeping. Help us keep the plant and shower rooms clean and orderly. Place waste material, paper, milk, bottles, etc., in the containers provided. Observe "No Smoking" signs.

7. Do not distract the attention of others by unnecessary shouting, catcalls, or loud or unexpected noises. A very dangerous situation might be created if other employees are distracted by such noise.

8. In case of accident or injury, contact a supervisor immediately.

Agreement
between
The ABC Company
and
Local 209, United Brotherhood of American Workers

Grievances, and Grievance Procedure

Article 5 (pertinent sections):

25. For the purposes of this Agreement, grievances are complaints which concern alleged violations of the contract.

26. Any grievances of any employee covered by the terms of this Agreement, or any dispute which shall arise between the Union or its members and the Company with respect to the interpretation or application of any of the terms or provisions of this Agreement, shall be determined, during the term of this Agreement, by the procedure set forth by this Article.

27. Notice of any grievance must be filed with the Company and with the Union committee within two (2) weeks after its occurrence or latest existence, providing such grievance is known to the aggrieved. The failure by either party to file the grievance within this time limitation shall be construed and be deemed to be an abandonment of the grievance.

28. An employee or group of employees who have a grievance may request that their immediate supervisor permit them to discuss their grievance with the union steward on duty at the time the grievance is placed. If an employee requests the presence of the steward, the employee's supervisor shall summon the steward as soon as possible, but not later than one (1) hour following such request, providing the steward or alternate steward is at work when such request is made. In the event the supervisor is not available at the time the employee desires to make such request, then the employee shall use the department phone to call the supervisor.

29. In requesting a steward, an aggrieved employee must state the nature of the grievance to the supervisor. However, the employee may wait for the arrival of the steward so requested before continuing the grievance discussion.

30. A grievance shall be handled as follows:

STEP 1. The matter will be discussed between the aggrieved employee and the immediate supervisor. The grievant, if desired, may have the steward join in the discussion. In such case, a higher level member of management may also join in the discussion as a Company representative. If the matter is not satisfactorily adjusted in such manner, then the matter will be reduced to writing by the employee's steward and signed and dated by the employee and the steward. The written grievance shall be handed to the supervisor who shall note thereon the date it is received. The supervisor will give a written answer not later than three (3) working days after receipt of the written grievance, or the grievance shall be deemed to have been granted by the company.

31. STEP 2. If not satisfactorily settled in Step 1, the steward may appeal the grievance to Step 2 by giving written notice to the supervisor within three (3) working days after receipt of the supervisor's written answer. If not appealed within said three (3) working-day period, the grievance shall be deemed to have been settled as answered by the supervisor. The grievance shall be discussed at the second step between the steward and members of the Negotiating Committee and a higher level manager of the Company and/or designee. The Company manager shall have three (3) working days following such meeting to give written answer to the Negotiating Committee, or the grievance shall be deemed to have been granted by the Company.

32. STEP 3. The grievance may be taken up with Management at the next regularly scheduled meeting with the Negotiating Committee, or if mutually agreed, a special meeting may be called. The International Representative may attend this meeting if desired.

In the event the union does not request in writing to appeal the grievance to the third step within five (5) working days following the Company manager's answer, the grievance shall be deemed to have been settled as answered by the Company manager. If a satisfactory settlement of a grievance discussed in this meeting is not reached, Management will give its written answer to the Chairperson of the Negotiating Committee (copy to International Representative) within five (5) working days following the final meeting, or the grievance shall be deemed to have been granted by the Company. Time limits, as specified herein, may be extended by mutual agreement in writing.

33. Regular meetings between the Negotiating Committee and the Company shall be held the first Tuesday of each month starting at 1:00 p.m. and ending at 3:00 p.m. or earlier. Unfinished business at 3:00 p.m. will be carried over to a meeting at 1:00 p.m. the following day, unless otherwise agreed upon. Meetings under this section shall be held when requested by the Union or the Company.

34. Any difference involving the meaning and application of any provisions of this Agreement that has not been satisfactorily settled in the foregoing steps of the grievance procedure shall be submitted to arbitration, provided that intention to arbitrate must be given in writing to the other party within ten (10) working days following conclusion of the 3d step of the grievance procedure or the matter will be closed. In the event the parties are unable to agree upon an arbitrator within five (5) working days after arbitration is invoked, they shall immediately and jointly request that the American Arbitration Association submit the names of five (5) persons qualified to act as arbitrators. If the parties cannot agree upon an arbitrator from the names of the original panel submitted, then the Company and the Union shall again jointly request the American Arbitration Association to submit a second panel of seven (7) persons qualified to act as arbitrators. Union and Company representatives shall each have the choice of alternately striking the names of three (3) of these seven (7) persons, and the remaining (or seventh) person shall be selected as the arbitrator. The arbitrator shall have jurisdiction and authority only to interpret and apply the provisions of this Agreement insofar as it be necessary to the determination of such grievance, and the arbitrator shall not have any jurisdiction or authority to alter, amend in any way, or add to the provisions of this Agreement. The decision of the arbitrator shall be final and binding on the Company, the Union, and the employees. The expense of the arbitrator shall be borne equally by the Union and the Company.

35.   A regular or the alternate steward serving in any of the above-mentioned capacities shall be compensated at the steward's base hourly rate for time expended in grievance negotiations during each such steward's regular working hours, and the Negotiating Committee shall be paid up to eight (8) hours per day for time spent on third step grievances and during labor contract negotiations.

36.   Officers and/or representatives of the International Union, United Brotherhood of American Workers (UBAW), may sit in on any regular or special meeting between the Company and the Negotiating Committee.

*   *   *

Suspension and/or Discharge

Article 14 (pertinent sections):

119.   In the exercise of its prerogatives as set forth in Article 2, the Company agrees to follow the principles of corrective discipline; the Company further agrees that an employee shall not be peremptorily discharged, but that in all instances in which the Company may conclude that an employee's conduct justifies discharge or suspension, the employee shall first be suspended by notice in writing, copy to the local Union, giving notification of the Company's intention to discharge. Such suspension shall be for not more than five (5) working days. During this period of initial suspension the employee may, if it is believed that he or she has been unjustly dealt with, make a request in writing to an executive of the Company for a hearing and a statement of the offense before the supervisor and/or executive of the Company. A member of the negotiating Committee may be present at such hearing. The facts concerning the case shall be made available to both parties. After such hearing, the Company may conclude that the employee be discharged or that the suspension be extended or revoked.

          If the suspension is revoked, the employee shall be returned to employment and receive full compensation at regular straight-time pay for the time lost, but in the event a disposition shall result in either the affirmation or extension of the suspension or discharge of the employee, the employee may allege a grievance which shall be handled in accordance with the procedures outlined in Article 5, Section 34. Final decision on all suspension and discharge cases shall be made by the Company within five (5) days from the date of filing of the grievance.

Should it be determined by an arbitration decision that the employee has been suspended or discharged unjustly, the Company shall reinstate the employee and pay full compensation at the employee's regular straight-time rate of pay for the time lost.

120. The Company may adopt reasonable plant rules. In the event new rules are adopted during the life of this Agreement, the Union will be notified two (2) weeks in advance of placing the rules in effect.

In imposing discipline on a current charge, the Company will not take into specific direct account any prior infraction which occurred more than two (2) years previously, and the employee's record will be cleared of any disciplinary action twenty-four (24) months after such action was taken.

Each employee will be given a copy of any warning, reprimand, suspension, or disciplinary layoff entered on the record within two (2) weeks of the alleged offense, provided such offense is known to the Company.

Forms on the following pages may be removed from this booklet and used as exhibits while playing the Game. Page numbers are shown as business form numbers in the lower left corner of the forms.

JOB DESCRIPTION

Job Title ___SET-UP MACHINIST___

Department ___Machine___

Duties Required:

1. Receives instructions, drawings, sketches, etc., from department supervision.
2. Performs all setups on assigned machines, selecting and installing appropriate tooling, speeds, feeds, etc.
3. Performs and/or instructs and assists Machinists in difficult and nonroutine setups on their units.
4. Checks, instructs, and assists Machinists in all operations, as required.
5. Lays off and drills material, as required.
6. Loads and unloads material from assigned machine manually or with the aid of a jib or floor-operated overhead crane.
7. Operates lathes, boring mills, grinders, planers, drill presses, etc., in all operations.
8. Grinds and sharpens all types of tooling, as required.
9. Operates cranes and other manual or mechanical equipment in moving material.
10. Instructs and checks work of operators, as necessary.
11. Performs or assists in performing machine repairs in Machine Department.

Tools and Equipment:

Lathes, planers, grinders, boring mills, drill presses, etc., micrometers, calipers, gauges, miscellaneous hand tools and measuring instruments.

Materials:

All types of metal--billets, bars, forgings, etc.

Source of Supervision: Machine Department

Responsibility to Direct Others:

On-the-job direction, assistance, and instruction to Machinists or other assigned help.

[The above statement reflects the general details considered necessary to describe the principal duties of the job identified, and shall not be construed as a detailed description of all the work requirements that may be inherent of the job.]

Described By ___Olen Smith___   Reviewed By ___Joan Williams___

Certificate of Award

This Certifies That

ROBERT M. JONES

In Recognition of Distinguished Achievement is

EMPLOYEE OF THE YEAR

and by Recommendation of the Committee on Awards has been Granted this Certificate.

Given at Evans, Michigan this 12th day of June 19 70

Richard M. Hanover, President

Allen W. Moskowitz, Vice President

THE ABC COMPANY

THE **ABC** COMPANY

Certificate of Appreciation

This certificate has been Awarded to

ROBERT M. JONES

In appreciation of

Twenty (20) Years of Distinguished Service

Given this 18th Day of ___January___ 19 72

Richard M. Hanover

President + Chief Executive Officer

The ABC Company
Report of Industrial Injury

Employee's Name: _____Robert Jones (#2084)_____   Date of Injury: _December 16, 1977_

Department: _____Machine_____   Time of Injury: _____9:20 p.m._____

Description of Injury and Treatment:

At around 9:20 p.m., Mr. Jones sustained an injury to his ribs after slipping off the platform on the #4 Bullard lathe. Jones was tightening the chuck when he either lost his footing on the oily platform, or his wrench slipped off the chuck. It is unknown whether his feet slipped or the wrench slipped first. When he lost his balance, he fell against the chuck.

Jones was assisted to my office by Hank Rains and Luis Lamas. Jones appeared dazed and confused. I detected a slight odor of alcohol on his breath. He appeared to be in control of his faculties. He refused medical treatment, and after resting for about a half hour returned to work for the remainder of his shift.

Dennis Cushing
Dennis Cushing
Supervisor

The ABC Company
Report of Industrial Injury

Employee's Name: _____Robert Jones (#2084)_____   Date of Injury: _____February 15, 1978_____

Department: _____Machine_____   Time of Injury: _____2:30 p.m._____

Description of Injury and Treatment:

At approximately 2:30 p.m., Robert Jones came to my office to report that he had bruised his hand after having dropped a steel bar on it. He was moving some finished work, and in the process a steel spindle weighing about 150 pounds fell over. He tried to stop the spindle from hitting the floor. He was unsuccessful in his efforts and the spindle fell on his hand.

When I observed his hand it was bruised and swollen. I also noticed a minor cut. Jones complained about the pain and did a lot of swearing. He was sent to the hospital where he received treatment. He did not return to work for two days.

Dennis Cushing
Dennis Cushing
Supervisor

The ABC Company
Report of Industrial Injury

Employee's Name: _____Robert Jones (#2084)_____   Date of Injury: __April 4, 1978__

Department: _____Machine_____   Time of Injury: ____2:00 p.m.____

Description of Injury and Treatment:

Shortly before 2 p.m., Robert Jones sustained an injury to his knee when he stepped backward off a stepladder. As he was falling to the ground, he twisted his knee on a rung of the ladder.

I was called to the scene of the accident. Jones was dazed and his speech was slurred. There was a strong odor of alcohol on his breath. He was in considerable pain and had to be taken to the hospital by ambulance. I issued a written warning for violation of general safety rules.

Dennis Cushing
Dennis Cushing
Supervisor

The ABC Company
Report of Industrial Injury

Employee's Name: _____Robert Jones (#2084)_____   Date of Injury: _April 19, 1978_

Department: _____Machine_____   Time of Injury: _____11:00 a.m._____

Description of Injury and Treatment:

At around 11 a.m., Mr. Jones sustained a lower back injury while attempting
to stop the forward momentum of a 1500-pound round steel bar that had been
placed on the floor after being removed from a lathe. For reasons unknown,
the bar started to roll. As it gained momentum, Jones ran in front of it
and attempted to stop it with his body. He contends that he exerted so
much force against the bar that he wrenched his back. Personally, I have
some doubts about the validity of his claim. The medical clinic where he
was treated after the injury noted in their report that there was no physical evidence of injury, although the patient complained profusely about
back pain.

In addition, I have another reason for questioning this injury. Jones had
told a number of employees that he needed some time off from work with pay
to take care of things around a number of rental properties he owns. However, no employee will give formal testimony about Jones' remarks.

Dennis Cushing
Dennis Cushing
Supervisor

Note: The company contested the Worker's Compensation claim on this injury.
        The company lost its appeal to the Worker's Compensation Review Board.

The ABC Company
Report of Industrial Injury

Employee's Name: _____ Robert Jones (#2084) _____   Date of Injury: _October 16, 1978_

Department: _____ Machine _____   Time of Injury: _____ 3:30 p.m. _____

Description of Injury and Treatment:

At approximately 3:30 p.m., Mr. Jones lacerated his left palm while attempting to wedge a used do-all hacksaw blade under the leg of a lathe. He was trying to use the blade as a shim to keep the lathe balanced. While he was trying to insert the blade between the bottom of the leg and the floor, his hand slipped and the teeth on the blade cut into his palm. He was taken to the medical clinic where he received treatment. He did not return to work the remainder of his shift.

Alfred Cisco
Alfred Cisco
Supervisor

The ABC Company
Report of Industrial Injury

Employee's Name: _____Robert Jones (#2084)_____   Date of Injury: _January 18, 1979_

Department: _____Machine_____   Time of Injury: _____Unknown_____

Description of Injury and Treatment:

I was not made aware of this injury until late in the afternoon on the 18th. Jones came to me stating that his wrist hurt. I inquired as to how and why this injury occurred. He claimed it happened in the morning when he was making some adjustments on the #7 engine lathe. He claimed that his grip slipped and he twisted his wrist. I did not observe any physical damage. He complained of severe pain and when I touched his wrist, he cried out because of the pain. I sent him to the medical clinic where the wrist was X-rayed and bandaged. The X rays showed no bone damage. There were no witnesses to his being injured.

Alfred Cisco
Alfred Cisco
Supervisor

The ABC Company
Report of Industrial Injury

Employee's Name: _____ Robert Jones (#2084) _____   Date of Injury: ___ April 30, 1979 ___

Department: _____ Machine _____   Time of Injury: _____ 9:30 a.m. _____

Description of Injury and Treatment:

At the start of the shift, Mr. Jones was assigned to realign the feed mechanism on the #2 Muller lathe. Jones made static adjustments to the feed
mechanism. Arnold King, the lathe operator, turned the lathe on so Jones
could make final adjustments. While the lathe was operating and cutting a
piece of work in process, some coolant with metal particles suspended in
the solution splashed into Jones' face. As a result, Jones sustained an
abrasion to his left eye. When I observed him at 9:30 a.m., his eye was
swollen. I could see a foreign body in it. He was sent to the medical
clinic where he received medical treatment. The physician reported that
there was no permanent damage to the eye. Jones took the remainder of the
day off from work.

Alfred Cisco
Alfred Cisco
Supervisor

The ABC Company
Report of Industrial Injury

Employee's Name: _____Robert Jones (#2084)_____   Date of Injury: _August 20, 1979_

Department: _____Machine_____   Time of Injury: _____8:00 p.m._____

Description of Injury and Treatment:

Mr. Jones, while attempting to recenter work in process, slipped and cracked a rib. The piece had shifted off center and was wedged against one of the cam locking lugs. Jones was using a pry bar to realign the piece when he lost his footing and fell into the end of the bar. He was taken to the hospital where X rays showed that he had cracked a rib. The accident was witnessed by Manny Cortex and Ed Swift.

Rick Albertson
Rick Albertson
Supervisor

The ABC Company
Report of Industrial Injury

Employee's Name: _____Robert Jones (#2084)_____   Date of Injury: _October 31, 1979_

Department: _____Machine_____   Time of Injury: _____1:30 p.m._____

Description of Injury and Treatment:

At approximately 1:30 p.m., Jones sustained a back injury after he slipped on a piece of flat metal. He was in the process of walking across the shop floor and slipped on a flat metal plate. When I observed him, he was incoherent, his speech was slurred, and his pupils were dilated. In addition, I could smell alcohol on his breath. He refused to lift himself from the floor, claiming that he was in too much pain to move. A stretcher was brought to him and he was taken to the hospital and X-rayed. The X rays showed no damage to his back or ribs.

Alfred Cisco
Alfred Cisco
Supervisor

Note: The company contested the Worker's Compensation claim on this injury.
The company lost its appeal to the Worker's Compensation Review Board.

The ABC Company
Report of Industrial Injury

Employee's Name: _____Robert Jones (#2084)_____ Date of Injury: _____December 3, 1979_____

Department: _____Machine_____ Time of Injury: _____Unknown_____

Description of Injury and Treatment:

Shortly after the beginning of the shift, Jones came to me and said that he injured his right foot after a piece of steel dropped on it. He took his shoe off and showed me his swollen and bruised foot. It appeared to me that the injury I observed was not of recent origin. In my opinion, the bruising of the foot was at least three days old. Jones said he was unable to work for the rest of the day because he was having difficulty walking. I assigned him to processing paperwork, but after an hour he complained so much about his sore foot that I sent him for medical treatment. He did not return to work.

Rick Albertson
Rick Albertson
Supervisor

The ABC Company
Report of Industrial Injury

Employee's Name: _____ Robert Jones (#2084) _____   Date of Injury: _____ January 21, 1980 _____

Department: _____ Machine _____   Time of Injury: _____ 2:30 p.m. _____

Description of Injury and Treatment:

At approximately 2:30 p.m., I was called to #7 lathe where I found Jones lying on his back. He claimed that he had fallen off the lathe while tightening the locking bolts. In my opinion, he was totally inebriated and his inability to move from the floor was caused by his being under the influence rather than by the injury. He was taken to the hospital where the results of the medical examination were that he had sustained a bruise to his back.

Sarah Engels
Sarah Engels
Supervisor

The ABC Company
Report of Industrial Injury

Employee's Name: ___Robert Jones (#2084)___   Date of Injury: ___September 16, 1980___

Department: ___Machine___   Time of Injury: ___Unknown___

Description of Injury and Treatment:

While walking across the shop floor, Jones tripped on a steel plate and fell to the floor. I observed his falling and, in my opinion, he did not trip over the plate. He purposely fell over it. When I approached him and asked him if he was all right, he complained of pains in his back and insisted that he be taken to the local hospital. He refused to allow any of his fellow workers to place him on a stretcher. We had to call the local ambulance service to have him removed from the floor. The attending physician's medical report indicated that there was no physical evidence of injuries other than injuries that he had received on other occasions.

Sarah Engels
Sarah Engels
Supervisor

The ABC Company
Disciplinary Action

Date: <u>November 25, 1977</u>

Employee Name and No.: Robert Jones (#2084)

Effective Date: November 25, 1977

Period: Five (5) Scheduled Work Days

Reason(s) For Disciplinary Action:

On November 22, 1977, you struck Fred Cook heavily in the mouth cutting his jaw seriously and causing profuse bleeding. This is against all common rules of conduct and against the Company Rules, especially rule D7. In view of this situation, pursuant to Article 14 of the Contract, you are hereby suspended for five (5) working days, beginning with the start of your shift on Monday. Your suspension is with the intent to consider you for discharge from employment with the company.

Robert Clark
Robert Clark, Manager
Machine Department

Copy Received:

Robert M. Jones   11/25/77
Employee   Date

Lillian Rattison   11/25/77
Steward   Date

TO: Mr. Frank J. Edwards
     Vice President, Human Resources

I hereby request a hearing on the Suspension With the Intent to Discharge given to me on November 25, 1977. I am exercising my rights pursuant to Articles 5 and 14 of the Contract.

Robert M. Jones
Robert M. Jones

November 26, 1977
Date

The ABC Company

Evans, Michigan 48616

Date: November 28, 1977

To: Robert M. Jones

From: Robert Clark, Manager, Machine Department

Ref: Suspension

On November 25, 1977, you were given a Suspension With Intent to Discharge because of seriously striking Fred Cook.

Pursuant to Article 14 of the Contract, you are hereby notified that your suspension shall be ended at the end of the workday on November 29, 1977. Your next scheduled workday shall be December 1, 1977.

You are hereby cautioned about the great seriousness of fighting, especially because the consequences may be final. Should you receive another warning of this nature, you will be discharged from employment.

Robert Clark
Robert Clark, Manager
Machine Department

Copy Received:

Robert M. Jones 11/28
Employee

Lillian Rattison 11/28
Steward

City of Evans

Police Department
Arrest Report

Arresting Officer's Name: _____ H. K. Henderson _____

Badge No.: ___783___   *Date of Arrest:* ___May 8, 1978___

Statement of Facts Concerning The Arrest:

At 2200 hours we were called to the Last Watering Hole Tavern on the report of a disturbance. Upon entering the tavern, we observed a Mr. Robert Jones behaving in an erratic and reckless manner. Specifically, he was holding a chair over his head, loudly using profane and abusive language, and threatening to kill everyone in the entire establishment. It was obvious to us that the man was not in full control of his faculties. He was swaying to and fro while swinging the chair and we observed foam around his mouth. When we approached him, he threw the chair at us. We dodged the chair and corralled Mr. Jones. He was placed under arrest for public disturbance and being under the influence of intoxicants.

Patrick T. Wyman, MD

310 Fox Place   **Evans, Michigan 48616**

May 15, 1978

Mr. Frank J. Edwards
Vice President, Human Resources
The ABC Company
Evans, MI 48616

Dear Mr. Edwards

This is to certify that Robert M. Jones is under my
care for severe nerves and indigestion. His wife
informs me that he is an alcoholic and is willing
to go to the Getaway Rehabilitation Center for dry-
ing out and rehabilitative therapy.

If it is within the scope of your personnel practices, I request that he be given a 30-day leave
of absence from work for this purpose.

Respectfully

Patrick T. Wyman

Patrick T. Wyman, M.D.

PTW/pt

cc Hon. Mabel E. Kimbel

Municipal Court

20 So. Pleasant St.
Evans, Michigan 48616

May 17, 1978

Mr. Frank J. Edwards
Vice President, Human Resources
The ABC Company
Evans, MI 48616

Dear Mr. Edwards

At the request of Mr. and Mrs. Jones, Dr. Wyman, Mr. Jones' personal physician, informed me that Jones has a drinking problem. Mr. Jones recognizes that his drinking problem is affecting his attendance and job performance. He knows that he needs help and is fearful of losing his job if he continues to drink to excess. I am trying to work with Dr. Wyman and Mr. and Mrs. Jones in solving some of his present problems.

I am not making any representation to you that Mr. Jones is an alcoholic, but I do feel that, like many people, he drinks too much from time to time. As Judge in this court, I have used the Getaway Rehabilitation Center on several occasions for cases concerning alcohol and drug abuse. It is very highly respected, and there have been good results for those who have attended.

I feel the recommended period of time at the rehabilitation center would be in this man's best interest, and ultimately would improve his ability to work for you as well as diminish some absenteeism.

Please be kind enough to review this matter and let me know if this is consistent with your employment practices.

With best regards

Mabel E. Kimbel

Mabel E. Kimbel, Judge
Municipal Court

MEK/ac

The ABC Company
Evans, Michigan 48616

May 25, 1978

Honorable Mabel E. Kimbel
Municipal Court
210 South Pleasant Avenue
Evans, MI 48616

Dear Judge Kimbel:

In reference to your letter of May 17, 1978, concerning Robert
M. Jones, this company is willing to grant a 30-day leave of
absence for the purposes of rehabilitation provided that he
gives us proof that he was in residence at the rehabilitation
center during the time that he has been granted the leave of
absence.

Very truly yours,

Frank J. Edwards

Frank J. Edwards
Vice President, Human Resources

FJE/jw

WARRANT
State of Michigan

To: *THE BAILIFF*

You are commanded to take the body of the within named _____ ROBERT M. JONES _____
before the Honorable Judge of the Municipal Court of the City of Evans, Michigan, forthwith to answer unto THE CITY OF EVANS or STATE OF MICHIGAN as charged in the affidavit hereto annexed, and to this writ make legal service and due return.

Margaret J. McLaughlin
(Deputy Clerk, Municipal Court, Evans, Michigan)

RETURN OF WARRANT

On _____ May 8, 1978 _____ *I served the defendant named in the foregoing Warrant.*
       (date)

H. K. Henderson
(Signature of Arresting Officer)

ENTRY

_____ ROBERT M. JONES _____ *standing before me, was informed*
of the charge, entered a Plea of: (Guilty)   Not Guilty   No Contest

Trial Date: _____ July 10, 1978 _____

Defendant was thereupon tried and from evidence presented, was found (GUILTY)   NOT GUILTY

I adjudged that a fine be paid in amount of: $ 350.00
Costs in the amount of: $ _____
Suspend: Fine $_____ Cost $ _____
Sentence to _____ days in jail. Suspend _____

<u>DISPOSITION OF CASE:</u>

```
Robert M. Jones has been found guilty of offenses out-
lined in the attached police report.  Mr. Jones is to
be fined $350 plus court costs.  In addition, he is to
pay for all damages done to the tavern during his melee.
```

Signed: R. W. Jamison
Date: July 10, 1978

Getaway Rehabilitation Center
Route 59
Dorian, Michigan 48239

Office of the Executive Director:

August 15, 1978

Mr. Frank J. Edwards
Vice President, Human Resources
The ABC Company
Evans, MI 48616

Dear Mr. Edwards:

I am writing to inform you of the results of our efforts to help Mr. Jones control his illness. Mr. Jones has made progress far beyond what we expected. Our staff worked intensively with him to help him understand the causes and effects of his illness.

In our opinion, Mr. Jones has made sufficient progress to be able to resume his normal job duties. We also feel that he is in control of his problem and that a recurrence is unlikely.

Sincerely,

Cecilia P. Slevin, M.D., Ph.D.
Director

CPS/ej

The ABC Company
Disciplinary Action

Date: <u>April 7, 1980</u>

Employee Name and No.: Robert M. Jones (#2084)

Effective Date: April 7, 1980

Period:

Reason(s) For Disciplinary Action:

On April 4, 1980, you told several employees that your supervisor said that it was alright to go home early. You told the company later that your supervisor didn't actually say anything. This was interference with supervision and a complete violation of company rule D5. For the above reason, you are given a First Written Warning.

You are hereby cautioned that should you again receive another warning of the same nature, you will subject yourself to a disciplinary suspension from work.

Robert Clark
Robert Clark, Manager
Machine Department

Copy Received:

Robert M. Jones 4/7/80
Employee   Date

Evelyn Stout 4/7/80
Steward   Date

The ABC Company
Employee Grievance

1st Step

Submit to Supervisor in Triplicate

Grievance # 8964

Local No. 209 Unit	Department Machine	Date April 9, 1980
Name of Aggrieved Employee ROBERT M. JONES	Classification Set-Up Machinist	Shift 2d

Contract Violation Article 6	Section 52	Local Agreement Violated (if any)	

Oral Discussion with Supervisor (date) April 9, 1980	Time 3:30 p.m.	Result of Discussion Negative

Detailed Reasons for Grievance

On April 7, 1980, Robert Jones was issued a First Written Warning pertaining to a violation of company rule D5. The warning is related to a group grievance filed by the Machine Department, concerning unfair and dangerous working conditions that was filed in the month of January. Jones feels that because of the severity of conditions that prevailed on the night of January 15, he should not be held liable for his actions. He also feels that employees that are in the union and have a copy of the contract should be held responsible for their own actions. Jones feels that there was no violation of company rule D5 on his part.

Specific Adjustment Requested

We seek the removal of this unjust warning from Jones' record.

Aggrieved's Signature *Robert M. Jones* 4/9/80	Steward's Signature *Evelyn Stout*
Received by Supervisor *Dennis Cushing* (date)	

Important: Supervisor involved should give disposition, date of disposition, and detailed reasons for the disposition.

Management's Response to this Grievance:

It is management's firm belief that Jones was issued a First Written Warning for just cause. This grievance is denied.

April 11, 1980

City of Evans
Fire Department
Emergency Squad Report

Name: Robert M. Jones	Time Called: 8:30 p.m.	Date: May 5, 1980

Type of Incident:
☐ Trauma ☐ Home ☐ Industrial ☒ Commercial

Emergency Location: Kraeger Store--Central Avenue	Position Found: Lying on back

Current Medications: Nerve Pills	Allergies: None

Blood Pressure: 110/90	Pulse Rate: 116	Respiratory Rate: 20 Normal

Nature of Emergency: Head and back injury sustained as a result of a fall.

Description of Injury and Treatment:

At 8:30 in the evening we were called to the scene of an injury at the local supermarket. We found a Mr. Robert M. Jones lying on the floor. He claimed that he had injured his lower back and the back of his head when he fell. He said that he was on medication and that he had taken morphine tablets earlier in the day. There was a strong odor of an alcoholic beverage on his breath. His vital signs were taken and a cervical collar was put on, and the subject was placed on a back board. He was transported to the local hospital. Mr. Jones' son arrived at the scene of the accident shortly before the subject was taken to the hospital. The son indicated that on May 1, 1977, his father had been in an automobile accident and that he was under treatment by a doctor.

(p-73)

Squad Personnel: _A. J. Stevens_

The ABC Company
Evans, Michigan 48616

SECOND STEP GRIEVANCE MEETING--May 6, 1980

1. Grievance No. 8773--Billie Hooper
    The union agrees to withdraw this grievance without prejudice.

2. Grievance No. 8887--Alice Griffin
    The union agrees to withdraw this grievance without prejudice.

3. Grievance No. 8964--Robert Jones
    The union agrees to withdraw this grievance without prejudice.

4. Grievance No. 533--Carlos Martinez
    Management agrees to pay Martinez $12.56 to settle this grievance. In the
    future, management will temporarily transfer the senior card holder to the
    truck driver classification or pay him the truck driver classification
    wage rate if management elects not to temporarily transfer the senior card
    holder.

5. Grievance No. 356--Leslie Meagin
    Management elected to keep the regular manipulator operator on the manipu-
    lator and not transfer the next senior card holder (Meagin) for two rea-
    sons: (1) Efficiency reasons as noted in Section 61E, Paragraph 2, of the
    Contract, and (2) To provide Fox with the best possible training under an
    experienced operator since he was awarded the position pursuant to Section
    77(5) of the Contract.

6. Grievance No. 357--John Hooke
    The union agrees to withdraw this grievance without prejudice based upon
    the fact that management has already paid another grievant on the same
    situation cited by Hooke in this grievance.

7. Grievance No. 8963--Tim Isles
    Management agrees to pay Isles for 15 hours straight time at his prevail-
    ing wage rate to settle this grievance.

Robert Clark
Robert Clark, Manager
Machine Department

Evelyn Stout
Evelyn Stout, Chief Steward

The ABC Company
Disciplinary Action

Date: ___May 8, 1980___

Employee Name and No.: Robert Jones (#2084)

Effective Date: May 8, 1980

Period: Suspension for Five (5) Days With Intent to Discharge

Reason(s) For Disciplinary Action:

Yesterday, May 7, 1980, you violated Company Rules numbers D5, D6, and C2 and you were sent home for the remainder of the day.

Misconduct of this nature cannot be condoned. For this reason, you are hereby notified that effective this date you are subject to a suspension for five (5) working days with the intent to discharge you from employment with this company pursuant to Article 14, Section 119, of the Contract.

Robert Clark
Robert Clark, Manager
Machine Department

Copy Received:

Robert M. Jones   5/8/80
Employee   Date

Sam Neilson   5/8/80
Steward   Date

TO: Frank J. Edwards
     Vice President, Human Resources

On May 8, 1980, I was suspended with the intention to discharge.
I hereby request a hearing as pursuant to my rights under
Article 14 of the Contract.

Robert M. Jones
Robert M. Jones

May 9, 1980
Date

The ABC Company
Evans, Michigan 48616

May 15, 1980

Mr. Robert M. Jones
18 South Broad Street
Evans, MI 48616

Dear Mr. Jones:

Pursuant to Article 14 of the Contract and the Letter of Suspension With Intent to Discharge given you on May 8, 1980, this letter is to advise you that the company has considered the evidence presented at the hearing of May 12, 1980, together with other records in evidence, and it has been concluded that effective with the date of this letter, you will be discharged from employment with this company.

It should be noted that time limits for this answer were extended by agreement with the union.

Sincerely,

Frank J. Edwards
Frank J. Edwards
Vice President, Human Resources

FJE:jw

(Sent by Certified Mail)
Return receipt received

The ABC Company
Employee Grievance

1st Step

Grievance # 2040

Local No. Unit	Department	Date
209	Machine	May 16, 1980

Name of Aggrieved Employee	Classification	Shift
ROBERT M. JONES	Set-Up Machinist	2d

Contract Violation	Section	Local Agreement Violated (if any)
Article 6	52	

Oral Discussion with Supervisor (date)	Time	Result of Discussion
May 9, 1980	3:30 p.m.	Negative

Detailed Reasons for Grievance

On May 6, 1980, I moved my tools and locker to the new machine building at the supervisor's request. On May 7, 1980, I came to the old machine building to get my paycheck. I am under heavy drugs at a doctor's request. I had also been drinking because I was in pain. I had no intention of working this day, but did not call in. I was ordered off company property by the department manager, Mr. Clark. I called my wife and sent her back to get my check. I did not damage any company property or threaten anyone. On May 8, I reported to work and was told that I was under Suspension With Intent to Discharge. On May 15, I was discharged from the company.

Specific Adjustment Requested

I request that I be returned to my job and be paid for all monies lost from May 10, 1980.

Aggrieved's Signature	Steward's Signature
Robert M. Jones 5/16/80	*Sam Nielson*
Received by Supervisor (date)	
Sarah Engels	

Important: Supervisor involved should give disposition, date of disposition, and detailed reasons for the disposition.

Management's Response to this Grievance:

The ABC Company
Evans, Michigan 48616

THIRD STEP GRIEVANCE MEETING--May 27, 1980

1. Grievance No. 356--Leslie Meagin
   As per the Second Step answer, management had justifiable reasons for not transferring Barrett. It has not been past practice, except by special agreement on the Press Operator's position, for the entire chain of employees who would have been upgraded by temporary transfer to be paid a differential wage rate.

2. Grievance No. 8885--Merlyn Doles
   Due to the facts and circumstances pertaining to this grievance, management agrees to pay Doles $25.74 to settle this grievance.

3. Grievance No. 360--John Hooke
   The union agrees to withdraw this grievance without prejudice.

4. Grievance No. 313--Maintenance Department
   Management does not believe that an increase in wage rates is warranted because the additional equipment referred to in this grievance is being maintained by additional personnel and overtime as required.

5. Grievance No. 2040--Robert Jones
   Management believes that, because of the seriousness of the offenses, he was discharged for just cause. Therefore, this grievance is denied.

Frank J. Edwards
Frank J. Edwards, Vice President
Human Resources

Evelyn Stout
Evelyn Stout, Chief Steward

June 2, 1980
Date

The ABC Company
Evans, Michigan 48616

SPECIAL THIRD STEP GRIEVANCE MEETING--Pertaining to Discharge
of Robert M. Jones

Grievance No. 2040

Management agrees to settle this grievance by converting Jones'
discharge to a 45-day disciplinary discharge without pay. In
settling this grievance, management will send Jones a letter by
Registered Mail outlining the offenses he committed which re-
sulted in the destroying of company property and the breaking
of numerous company policies and rules. Jones' reinstatement
is based solely on his seniority with the company and settlement on that basis is a pure admission of Jones to the offenses
cited in his Letter of Discharge and the enclosed letter. This
disciplinary suspension will remain in his personnel file for
two years from the date of his suspension..

Frank J. Edwards
Frank J. Edwards, Vice President
Human Resources

Evelyn Stout
Evelyn Stout, Chief Steward

_____June 11, 1980_____
Date

The ABC Company

Evans, Michigan 48616

June 11, 1980

Mr. Robert M. Jones
18 South Broad Street
Evans, MI 48616

Dear Mr. Jones:

On May 7, at approximately 3:30 p.m., you reported to work at
the Machine Department. Members of management, as well as your
fellow employees, observed that you appeared to be highly intoxicated. Management spoke with you and in the ensuing hour
and one half you willfully destroyed company property by smash-
ing a toilet with a steel spindle, used foul and abusive language, and endangered the lives of personnel in the plant.
You were asked to leave the company premises and were told not
to return until the following day. You were also informed that
you were subject to disciplinary action because of your behavior.

At approximately 7:30 p.m., you returned to the company, still
in an intoxicated condition, and entered the plant under the
pretense of getting a paycheck from your supervisor. You were
ordered by your supervisor to leave the premises.

Your hostile behavior caused you to break company rules D5, D6,
B4, C2, and C3. As a result of your behavior, you were Suspended With the Intent to Discharge on the following day. A
suspension hearing was held and management made the decision to
discharge you from the company. The union appealed your discharge and argued persuasively on your behalf. As a result of
the union's persuasive arguments that you will change your behavior and because of the seniority that you have accrued with
the company, your discharge has been converted to a 45-day disciplinary suspension without pay.

Management fully expects that when you return to work you will be
committed to working under the company rules. Management must
forewarn you that if you break any company rule in the future,
especially any of those cited in this letter, you will be subject
to disciplinary action up to and including discharge.

Sincerely,

Frank J. Edwards

Frank J. Edwards
Vice President, Human Resources

FJE/jw
(Sent by Certified Mail)
Return Receipt Received

The ABC Company
Employee Grievance

1st Step

Submit to Supervisor in Triplicate

Grievance # 2169

Local No. Unit 209	Department Machine	Date October 3, 1980

Name of Aggrieved Employee JIM PHILLIPS	Classification Machinist	Shift 2d

Contract Violation Article 8	Section Par. 69	Local Agreement Violated (if any)	

Oral Discussion with Supervisor (date) October 3, 1980	Time 8:00 a.m.	Result of Discussion Negative

Detailed Reasons for Grievance

On October 3, 1980, Jim Phillips was assigned a job in the Machine Department by his supervisor. The job consisted of boring 1/16" out of a taper lock for a gear drive on one of the furnaces. This was not production work and was a relatively complex job for a low seniority machinist to perform. Phillips did receive some verbal instructions but not enough to complete the work task that was assigned. We feel that Phillips performed in the Set-Up Machinist classification—the taper lock had to be true within 15 thousandths of an inch tolerance. Management is trying to force relatively unskilled machinists to do complex work at a minimum wage. We will not accept such standards.

Specific Adjustment Requested

The union requests 2½ hours of pay at Set-Up Machinist's wage rate, which is the amount of time he spent on the taper lock. This is pursuant to Section 69 of the Contract.

Aggrieved's Signature *Jim Phillips* 10/3/80	Steward's Signature *David Samuelson*

Received by Supervisor *Sarah Engels* (date)	

Important: Supervisor involved should give disposition, date of disposition, and detailed reasons for the disposition.

Management's Response to this Grievance:

The ABC Company
Evans, Michigan 48616

SECOND STEP GRIEVANCE MEETING--October 7-8, 1980

1. <u>Grievance No. 4384--Harold Gordan</u>
   Management believes that there was just cause for taking disciplinary action against Gordan. Therefore, this grievance is denied.

2. <u>Grievance No. 89--Diane Smith</u>
   Pursuant to Section 92, Paragraph 2, of the Contract, Smith was denied holiday pay because she reported to work one hour and 51 minutes after the start of her scheduled workday. Therefore, this grievance is denied.

3. <u>Grievance No. 2169--Jim Phillips</u>
   Management agrees to pay Phillips $22.50 to settle this grievance. The settlement of this grievance is based upon the fact that Phillips, after requesting assistance from the Set-Up Machinist, did not receive proper instructions. The settlement of this grievance does not set any precedent.

4. <u>Grievance No. 543--Julie Gordan</u>
   The union agrees to withdraw this grievance without prejudice.

5. <u>Grievance No. 2166--Frank Burner</u>
   In cases where discharged employee's position has been awarded to another employee and the discharged employee is reinstated by a grievance settlement, the discharged employee is returned to his classification and the employee who had been awarded the position is bumped and returned to his previous classification. Therefore, this grievance is denied.

6. <u>Grievance No. 2163--Mike Garvey</u>
   Management's policy in assigning work to employees is to utilize employee's best skills and therefore operate the company in a manner that does not waste resources. In this case, management acted in the best interests of all parties. No discrimination was intended. Therefore, this grievance is denied.

Robert Clark
Robert Clark, Manager
Machine Department

Evelyn Stout
Evelyn Stout, Chief Steward

SWORN STATEMENT

OF

JIM PHILLIPS

I, Jim Phillips, voluntarily make the following sworn statement:

I filed grievance number 2169. It involved Robert Jones because he had not assisted me like he should have. The next day, October 4, 1980, Jones and Richard Ball came up to me while I was in the locker room. Jones told Ball to tell me what he (Jones) had done to guys who mess around with him. Ball said, "He will take care of you just like the treatment Doles got." Jones then said to me that if I ever used his name again there would be a $100 price on my hide. He made other threatening remarks which I don't recall.

I went to my machine and a short while later Jones came up to me and put his hand on my shoulder. He said, "You don't ever mention my name to any of the supervisors. If you want anything, come to me. I run this department, not the supervisors. Keep your mouth shut and nothing will happen to you." I looked down because I felt something sharp against my stomach. Jones was pressing a knife blade against me. He then said, "You keep your mouth shut or I will lay you wide open, or have it done to you, one of the two." He went on about how he had done it to others who caused problems. He then walked away.

Sometime later, while doing some work, a steel chip hit me in the eye. I was walking to my supervisor's office to have her take it out when Jones came up to me and said, "What's the matter?" I told him and he said, while pulling his knife out of his pocket, "Here, I'll take care of that." I ran to my supervisor's office. Jones followed me into the office. While my supervisor, Sarah Engels, was washing out my eye, Jones showed her some spent .38 caliber cartridges saying that he had found them out in the plant.

After I had returned to my machine, Jones again came over to me. He showed me some hollow point .38 caliber cartridges and said that he had shot at someone the other night but could not remember who it was. He further told me that he "had a gun in his toolbox and would use it if it became necessary."

I shut my machine off and immediately went to Sarah's office. I told her that I was quitting because some of the guys were pushing too hard.

I know Jones was drinking that day. I have seen him drink on the job many times. He keeps a fifth in his truck. He goes out there and fills a soda pop can with liquor and then takes it back to work with him. He gives everyone he does not like trouble. I do not like him. I am afraid of him.

Jim Phillips

Jim Phillips
October 13, 1980

(Notarized and witnessed by
 Frank Edwards and Robert Clark)

The ABC Company
Disciplinary Action

Date: <u>October 27, 1980</u>

Employee Name and No.: Robert M. Jones

Effective Date: October 27, 1980

Period: Suspension for Five (5) Days With Intent to Discharge

Reason(s) For Disciplinary Action:

The company has positive evidence that you are again breaking company rule D5 and others.

Management forewarned you in its letter to you of June 11, 1980, that if you broke these company rules in the future you would be subject to disciplinary action up to and including discharge.

Serious misconduct of this nature cannot be condoned. For this reason, you are hereby notified that effective this date, you are made subject to a suspension for five (5) working days with intent to discharge you from the employment of this company pursuant to Article 14, Section 119, of the Contract.

Robert Clark
Robert Clark, Manager
Machine Department

Copy Received:

<u>*Robert M. Jones*</u>   <u>10/27/80</u>
Employee   Date

<u>*Sam Nielson*</u>   <u>10/27/80</u>
Steward   Date

TO: Frank J. Edwards
      Vice President, Human Resources

I request a hearing on Section 119 of the Contract for the suspension given to me on October 27, 1980.

                                    Robert M. Jones
                              Robert M. Jones

                                    October 28, 1980
                              Date

The ABC Company
Evans, Michigan 48616

October 29, 1980

Mr. Robert M. Jones
18 South Broad Street
Evans, MI 48616

Dear Mr. Jones:

This is to inform you that pursuant to Article 14 of the Contract, all the facts of your case arising in connection with the Suspension and Intention to Discharge given you October 27, 1980, have been considered, and it has been determined that, effective this date, you are to be discharged from the employment of this company.

Very truly yours,

Robert Clark

Robert Clark, Manager
Machine Department

RC/jw

(Sent by Certified Mail)
Return Receipt Received

The ABC Company
Employee Grievance

1st Step

Submit to Supervisor in Triplicate

Grievance # 2008

Local No. Unit 209	Department Machine	Date October 30, 1980
Name of Aggrieved Employee ROBERT M. JONES	Classification Set-Up Machinist	Shift 2d
Contract Violation Article 2	Section Local Agreement Violated (if any)	
Oral Discussion with Supervisor (date) October 28, 1980	Time 10:00 a.m.	Result of Discussion Negative

Detailed Reasons for Grievance

On October 27, 1980, I was given a Suspension With the Intent to Discharge. And on October 29, 1980, I was discharged from the employment of this company for unjust reasons. The company said I broke rule D5. This is not true. I did not threaten anyone. Jim Phillips quit this company on October 4, 1980. I had no trouble with him. I treated the boy like a son while he worked under me. An operator in the plating room said that when Phillips was under him whenever he told Phillips to do something, he would think he was mad at him. Phillips was not a good employee. I tried my best to get him to do a better job. He is immature.

Specific Adjustment Requested

I request to be placed back on my job with all back pay and all my seniority.

Aggrieved's Signature *Robert M. Jones* 10/30/80	Steward's Signature *Lillian Rattison*
Received by Supervisor *Dennis Cushing* (date)	

Important: Supervisor involved should give disposition, date of disposition, and detailed reasons for the disposition.

Management's Response to this Grievance:

The ABC Company

Evans, Michigan 48616

THIRD STEP GRIEVANCE MEETING--November 18, 1980

1. Grievance No. 2005--Harold Gordan
   Based on the particular facts and circumstances pertaining to this case, management has reinstated Gordan with full seniority to his last position with the company. Management agrees to pay Gordan at his prevailing wage rate for all time lost less three (3) days that have passed since he broke seniority under Section 43C of the Contract. A second warning indicating a three (3) day disciplinary layoff for no reports will be placed in Gordan's personnel file. The settlement of this grievance does not set any precedent.

2. Grievance No. 2008--Robert Jones
   Management has reviewed the facts and circumstances pertaining to this grievance along with the record of disciplinary action taken against Jones this year. The seriousness of this violation of company rules, coupled with other recent disciplinary action taken against Jones, is, in management's opinion, "just cause" for sustaining his discharge from the company.

3. Grievance No. 4430--Charles Hilby
   The union agrees to withdraw this grievance without prejudice.

4. Grievance No. 4480--Benji Eto
   The union agrees to withdraw this grievance without prejudice.

5. Grievance No. 2010--Everett Gordon and Jean Futz
   Management agrees to settle this grievance by paying George Sipert for 1½ hours ($10.50) straight time at his prevailing wage rate. Management also agrees to pay Fred Tamton for 2½ hours ($1.03) the difference between his prevailing wage rate and $0.10 below the top utility worker's wage rate. Kurt Holdman, John Bolt, Jean Futz, Everett Gordon, and Tanya Croach will be paid temporary transfer wage rate differentials for 2½ hours each. The settlement of this grievance does not set any precedent.

Frank J. Edwards
Frank J. Edwards, Vice President
Human Resources

Evelyn Stout
Evelyn Stout, Chief Steward

City of Evans

Police Department
Arrest Report

Arresting Officer's Name: ___R. W. Reasoner___

Badge No.: __610__   Date of Arrest: __February 6, 1981__

Statement of Facts Concerning The Arrest:

At 1500 hours on February 6, 1981, Patrolman
Ethel Lumberger and this officer were dis-
patched to investigate the report of a motor-
ist driving on State Route 85 in an erratic
manner. We turned on our lights indicating
that the driver should pull over. He did not
respond and we used the siren to get his attention. We approached the suspect with caution and ordered him out of the automobile.
He refused to get out of the automobile and
used considerable profanity to express his
objection. He was ordered out at gunpoint,
and a thorough search of his person and the
automobile revealed that the driver's name
was Robert M. Jones. There was a strong odor
of alcohol about Mr. Jones and he was barely
coherent. We administered standard tests for
determining sobriety and both of us observed
that he could not pass any of them. He was
arrested for driving under the influence of
alcohol.

(p-107)